MAPUTO TI

GUIDE 2024:

Discovering Maputo's hidden gems with practical tips and safety

Dave C. Albert

Table of Contents

Chapter 1

Introduction to Maputo

Greetings from Maputo

Welcome to Maputo, the energetic capital of Mozambique! Maputo, tucked away along the Indian Ocean, is a mesmerizing fusion of vibrant

marketplaces, historic elegance, and a diverse range of cultures. Walking through the city's streets, you'll come across a mix of colonial-era buildings and contemporary constructions that showcase the nation's changing character.

Maputo's varied background is reflected in its vibrant cultural scene. Take a tour of the busy markets, such as the Feira Popular, where a sensory feast of local goods and spices may be experienced via their colors, noises, and fragrances. The city is home to a flourishing art scene, with galleries showing the creations of Mozambican artists that provide a window into the spirit of the country.

Maputo's food is a pleasant gastronomic excursion that draws inspiration from Indian, African, and Portuguese cooking traditions. The distinctive aromas of traditional matapa and the aromatic grilled prawns known as peri-peri are just two examples of how Mozambique's diverse cuisine celebrates its rich cultural heritage.

The city's beaches, such as Costa do Sol, provide a peaceful haven where golden sands and mild Indian Ocean seas meet for visitors looking to unwind. Enjoy a leisurely walk along Maputo's waterfront promenade, which offers stunning views of the ocean and the famous Iron House, which is a tribute to the city's architectural charm.

History buffs will be fascinated by sites like the Maputo Central Train Station, an architectural marvel that reflects the city's history, and the Fortaleza de Maputo, a fortification that dates back to the colonial period. These locations act as a narrative thread uniting Maputo's dynamic history and present.

Maputo's vibrant nightlife comes alive as the sun sets over the city. Experience the city's after-hours charm with a wide range of alternatives, from vibrant pubs with traditional Marrabenta music to chic rooftop clubs with panoramic views.

Essentially, Maputo extends a warm welcome to you and invites you to fully experience its alluring mix of culture, history, and scenic beauty. Whether you're interested in history, fine dining, or just want to have a different kind of adventure, Maputo guarantees an experience that will stay with you long after you leave its borders.

An overview of Maputo

Mozambique's capital city, Maputo, beckons with a certain appeal derived from its rich cultural heritage and historical importance. Situated on the stunning Indian Ocean coast, the city's streets tell an intriguing tale by combining colonial-era architecture with the energy of a contemporary African metropolis.

The bustling marketplaces that dot Maputo's landscape are irresistible. Particularly during the Feira Popular, the vibrant local crafts and the commotion of merchants combine to offer a very intense sensory experience. Here, the scents of local spices resonate in the air, pulsating at the center of Mozambique's cultural identity.

Maputo's emerging art scene is a haven for art lovers. Galleries display the skill of regional artists and provide a window into the changing stories that define Mozambique's character and spirit. The city takes on the appearance of a canvas, and every artistic brush enhances the vibrant cultural landscape.

Maputo's culinary discovery is a journey in itself. The blending of Indian, African, and Portuguese influences results in a wide variety of tastes. Maputo's food celebrates the history and richness of the country on a plate, from the delicious aroma of sizzling peri-peri prawns to the cozy embrace of matapa.

The shore of Maputo is a sanctuary for rest seekers. The Indian Ocean's rhythmic waves and the golden beaches of Costa do Sol provide for a tranquil setting. The city's beaches provide a getaway from the bustle of the city, beckoning residents and guests to relax in front of the stunning coastline view.

Maputo, a city rich in history, welcomes you to explore its architectural legacy. A testimony to the city's history is the Fortaleza de Maputo, a stronghold from the colonial period, and the Maputo Central Train Station is an architectural marvel that tells the tale of Mozambique's development.

When the sun sets, Maputo becomes a vibrant playground. The city's nightlife offers something for everyone, so every evening is an exciting new experience, whether you like the sophisticated rooftop lounges with panoramic views or the lively sounds of marrabenta music in traditional taverns.

Maputo is essentially a city that melds its modern character with its ancient foundations in a seamless manner. Maputo invites you to experience the spirit of Mozambique's capital city, whether you're exploring its streets, savoring its cuisine, or just taking in the breathtaking views of its coastline.

Climate and Geography

Maputo's topography is a mesmerizing waltz between land and sea, since it lies tucked away along the sapphire-blue waves of the Indian Ocean. The city, which is in Mozambique's southern region, is strategically placed along the nation's coastline. You will experience a wonderful fusion of urban developments, lush foliage, and the rhythmic waves that hug its coastline as you travel across its diversified terrain.

The climate of Maputo is a tropical savanna with distinct wet and dry seasons. The city has a beautiful equilibrium all year round, with temperatures often ranging from moderate to hot. November to April are the rainy seasons. During this time, cool showers replenish the soil and intensify the hues of the surrounding vegetation.

The topography of the city gives its landscape a dynamic touch. The interior parts show rolling hills and patches of flora, while the coastal sections have immaculate beaches and expansive views of the ocean. This geographic variety adds to the city's attraction by providing a variety of experiences for both locals and tourists.

Maputo's climate is significantly shaped by the Indian Ocean, which affects both temperature and precipitation patterns. Especially in the warmer months, the sea breeze's natural cooling impact offers relief from the heat of the tropical climate. The city's environment is defined by its closeness to the coast, which also offers options for water-based recreation and a charming setting for strolls along the shore.

Maputo's topography influences the city's economic activity in addition to serving as a scenic canvas. With its advantageous location along the coast, the port of Maputo is an important entry point for international commerce, promoting economic expansion and ties to the rest of the world.

In conclusion, Maputo's terrain is varied, its temperature oscillates between tropical warmth and refreshing showers, and its seaside beauty all work well together. Whether you're attracted to the vibrant urban core of this alluring Mozambican city, the verdant interior hills, or the sandy beaches, this is a place that begs for exploration.

Chapter 2

Means of Getting to Maputo

Traveling by air to Maputo

When thinking about flying to Maputo, there are a few things to consider that might make the trip smooth and pleasurable. Selecting an airline that fits travel schedules, economic restrictions, and personal preferences is the first step towards starting this adventure. Examining the evaluations of various carriers may provide important information about the quality of service, available features, and general consumer happiness.

Booking the flight is the next crucial step after choosing the airline. This procedure may be made easier by using internet resources or travel agents, which enable users to evaluate costs, flight times, and stopover choices. It's important to take into account things like layovers and transit times since they may have a big influence on the whole trip.

Careful planning is necessary when the travel date draws near. It is crucial to verify the flight information, make sure that your travel papers are valid, and follow any special instructions that the airline or location may have. A hassle-free trip is also facilitated by packing effectively, which includes bringing along the things you really need for your trip and following baggage guidelines.

One common but crucial part of flying is getting through security and check-in processes when you get to the airport. A seamless transition through these procedures is ensured by being acquainted with the airport layout and adhering to airline personnel instructions.

After boarding, travelers may take their seats and look forward to their flying experience. Every passenger has different interests when it comes to what they want to do on their trip, whether it be eating onboard, watching movies on the plane, or just lounging around the window seat and soaking in the expansive vistas.

Passengers are treated to amazing overhead views that give them a peek at the city's stunning coastline and scenery as the plane reaches Maputo. A breathtaking view opens up as you descend into Maputo International Airport, preparing you for the experiences that lie ahead in this energetic metropolis.

To sum up, traveling to Maputo by plane requires a careful process that includes choosing an airline, scheduling a trip, getting ready for departure, going through airport security, and enjoying the in-flight experience. Since every stage of the trip adds to the whole experience, flying is a necessary component of exploring and learning about Maputo's beauty and attractiveness.

Maputo International Airport

Situated on Africa's southeast coast, Maputo International Airport serves as the main entry point to the vibrant and culturally diverse capital city of Mozambique. This important center, also known as Mavalane International Airport, is the first port of call for tourists and a well-known landmark for locals returning home.

Travelers are greeted by the airport's charming architecture and contemporary facilities upon arrival, which sets the tone for their stay in Maputo.

The terminal's architecture is a visually pleasing introduction to the lively environment that lies beyond its gates, reflecting the city's fusion of modern and colonial elements.

The check-in procedure, which is a prelude to the journey that awaits travelers, proceeds smoothly within the busy airport. A seamless transition from the pleasure of discovery to the anticipation of departure is ensured by attentive airport workers who help with process navigation.

Even though they are regular, security checks are carried out effectively, putting passenger safety first and preserving a welcoming atmosphere for travelers. Because of the airport's dedication to security, travelers can feel confident and concentrate on the exciting discoveries they will make in Maputo rather than worrying about how they will get there.

The duty-free shops and restaurants at Maputo International Airport give travelers a chance to sample some of Mozambique's wide range of products. The airport's shopping areas provide a glimpse of the nation's diverse culture, ranging from internationally renowned brands to handcrafted gifts made locally. Restaurants provide you with delectable food that serves as an introduction to the tastes that characterize Mozambican cuisine.

For those lucky enough to get a window seat, the airport's strategic position next to the Indian Ocean provides stunning vistas during takeoff and landing, making for unforgettable experiences. The airport's role as a regional transit center is reflected in its broad runway, which can accommodate a variety of aircraft.

Travelers may easily go from flying to the center of Maputo's busy streets thanks to effective ground transportation alternatives that link the airport to different sections of the city. For a variety of tastes and travel plans, flexible options, including taxis, shuttles, and rental automobiles, are available.

Maputo International Airport is essentially a logistical entry point as well as a forerunner to the natural, historical, and cultural treasures that lie ahead in Maputo. For tourists coming by flight, its blend of practicality, visual appeal, and local importance perfectly captures the essence of Mozambique, making it an essential component of the trip.

Getting to Maputo via Land

A land trip to Maputo offers a unique travel experience that lets travelers enjoy the shifting scenery, engage with the local way of life, and observe the environment's slow evolution. This journey is greatly influenced by the kind of transportation that is selected, which offers alternatives from the private vehicle's liberating drive to the bus's steady hum.

If you choose to travel by bus or coach, the trip is experienced as a group adventure, with other travelers acting as temporary co-stars in the road story. Every mile of the journey to Maputo adds a new chapter to the ever-changing landscape outside the window, which showcases the varied landscape of Mozambique, from beautiful farmland to a busy city.

Alternatively, driving the distance offers a distinct feeling of independence. The vast road stretches out before you, offering unexpected discoveries and side trips to unearthed treasures. The drive becomes an immersive experience as the car winds through small towns and roads, letting passengers take in the sights, sounds, and scents of Mozambique's rural landscapes.

Traveling through border crossings adds a sense of excitement as the joy of entering a new country triumphs over bureaucratic procedures. Gradually, the language, architecture, and even the state of the roads change, marking the changing terrain and pointing the way toward the colorful cultural tapestry that awaits in Maputo.

The rest spots along the way provide chances to interact with local populations in addition to providing a means of physical rest. Roadside markets provide a rainbow of hues and tastes, enticing visitors to explore local specialties and purchase handcrafted goods, strengthening their connection with Mozambique's rich cultural legacy.

The pulse of the city becomes noticeable as the drive gets closer to Maputo. Travelers are enveloped by traffic patterns, subtle architectural details, and the city's spirit as they arrive at the conclusion of a land trip that goes beyond simple conveyance. Traveling by land turns into an essential component of the experience, setting the stage for fully immersing oneself in Maputo's unique fusion of culture, history, and modernity.

Land transportation to Maputo is, in essence, more than just a means of transportation. This trip captures the spirit of the journey itself, providing a rich tapestry of encounters that deepen the visitor's connection to Mozambique's varied landscapes and the energetic Maputo community.

Route by road from Maputo to South Africa

Traveling by car from South Africa to Maputo is an enthralling journey that takes you through the several types of scenery that characterize the southern part of Africa. The sound of tires chugging down South African roads heralds the trip's eventual shift from the busy metropolis to the wide-open spaces of the countryside.

The excitement level increases when one crosses into Mozambique because of the change in landscape and the slight cultural difference. As the smooth ribbon of asphalt unfolds, it leads drivers past charming towns and villages and provides a window into the everyday lives of the people who live there and whose tales are woven into the very fabric of the road.

The scenery changes dramatically as the tour goes on, going from the lush, tropical foliage of Mozambique to the dry beauty of South Africa. The voyage becomes a beautiful symphony as the surroundings' shifting colors represent the abundant biodiversity that this part of Africa is known for.

Roadside markets dotted along the route to Maputo provide a variety of fruits, handicrafts, and regional delicacies from vendors. These rest spots provide a chance to stretch one's legs as well as interact with the rich cultural tapestry of Mozambique and sample the distinctive cuisine of the area.

As you drive through Maputo's suburbs, the city begins to come into view. The route smoothly melds into Maputo's vibrant street rhythm as the city's pulse quickens. The building, which is a blend of contemporary and colonial styles, tells the tale of the city's past and sets the scene for the exciting journey that lies within its walls.

Traveling by road from South Africa to Maputo is more than simply a way to go from place to place; it's a story that develops with each kilometer. It's about the unexpected discoveries made along the route, the friendships made along the way, and the slow revelation of Maputo's charms. It's evidence for the theory that the real meaning of travel is found in the tales carved into the routes that go there as well as the actual destinations.

Public Transport

In Maputo, public transit is an energetic and essential part of everyday life, winding through the streets like a lively tapestry to link the city's many communities. The chapa, or minibus taxis, which are a common sight in Maputo's urban environment and are known for their loud music and vivid colors, serve as the system's backbone. They are symbolic of the city's lively atmosphere.

Getting aboard a chapa is like diving right into the heart of the city. A symphony of urban life is created by the dance of commuters getting on and off the train, the rhythmic flow of coins being exchanged, and the vibrant chatter amongst passengers. Every chapa route narrates a different tale as it passes by thriving marketplaces, old neighborhoods, and contemporary constructions, providing an insight into Maputo's complex personality.

The chapa transforms into a moving microcosm of Maputo's cultural variety as it travels through the city's streets. The little area shared by passengers from all backgrounds encourages a feeling of social harmony. Not only is it a way to go about it, but it's also a place where people congregate and temporarily exchange tales while traveling together.

Maputo's public transport network goes beyond chapas to include the famous dhow boats that ferry people across the bay, offering a convenient and picturesque connection between the busy city center and the more laid-back Katembe neighborhood. In the center of the city, a unique marine sensation is created by the boat's swing, the sea wind, and the expansive views of Maputo's cityscape.

Maputo has an extensive bus network that runs throughout the city, offering a practical and reasonably priced way to get about for an everyday commute for those looking for a more regimented form of transportation. The buses, decked up in colorful artwork, are moving canvases that convey the creative flare of the city while effectively getting people where they need to go.

There are difficulties with Maputo's public transit system. The tale includes elements such as traffic congestion, timetable variations, and occasional unpredictability. But these peculiarities add to the genuineness of the journey, turning a normal commute into an exciting journey through Maputo's vibrant and always-changing metropolitan environment.

In Maputo, public transportation has purposes beyond simple commuting. It's a vibrant portrayal of the city's personality and a group excursion around the vibrant center of Mozambique's capital. Every kind of transportation, whether it be the organized efficiency of a city bus, the rhythmic bounce of a chapa, or the soft swing of a dhow boat, adds to the colorful mosaic that is Maputo's public transportation system.

Chapter 3

Accommodation Options in Maputo

The Best Resorts and Hotels in Maputo

Mozambique's bustling metropolis, Maputo, is home to a number of excellent hotels and resorts that can accommodate a wide variety of demands and tastes. The Polana Serena Hotel is a famous institution with a long history that dates back to the 1920s and is considered one of the city's hospitality jewels. Offering visitors an opulent experience in a scenic location, this opulent hideaway skillfully combines colonial charm with contemporary luxury.

In search of a chic and modern setting, the Radisson Blu Hotel Maputo is a notable choice. This luxurious hotel offers the perfect combination of luxury and convenience, with breathtaking views of the ocean and a prominent position. It is a popular option for both business and leisure tourists because of its luxurious rooms and suites and first-rate services.

Discover the White Pearl Resorts on the immaculate beachfront of Ponta Mamoli, a destination worth visiting if seclusion and peace are your top priorities. This five-star resort, which offers private villas, fine dining, and a variety of water sports among stunning coastline scenery, is known for its barefoot luxury.

Situated on a hill with a view of Maputo Bay, the Cardoso Hotel is an additional interesting choice. It appeals to those looking for a stylish but inviting atmosphere with its expansive views and dedication to providing exceptional service. The hotel's decor and menu reflect the blending of Portuguese and Mozambican traditions.

Mozambique's cultural diversity is embodied at Southern Sun Maputo, where visitors may experience a seamless fusion of regional customs and global benchmarks. This hotel's central location makes it a great starting point for seeing Maputo's thriving historical monuments, markets, and cultural scene.

Maputo's selection of premier hotels and resorts guarantees a varied and unforgettable stay for discriminating guests, regardless of their preferences for modern elegance, historical grandeur, or tranquil beach getaways.

Opulent lodging

Travelers are drawn to Maputo, the vibrant city of Mozambique, by its array of lavish lodging options that redefine what it means to live in luxury. The Polana Serena Hotel, an architectural marvel that skillfully blends traditional elegance with contemporary conveniences, is in the vanguard of this pleasure. This storied hotel provides luxurious accommodations, fine food, and a spa experience that goes beyond mere relaxation.

When it comes to modern elegance, the Radisson Blu Hotel Maputo is a shining example of refinement. This elegant facility, which has an excellent view of the Indian Ocean, offers the ideal balance of comfort and sophistication. Luxurious accommodations, cutting-edge amenities, and flawless service combine to create an ambiance of sophisticated elegance, making it a top pick for discriminating tourists.

Go a little further, and you'll come to Ponta Mamoli's White Pearl Resorts, which are quite magical. This remote haven, tucked away along the immaculate shoreline, is the pinnacle of barefoot luxury. Each of the private villas has a plunge pool and is well designed. White Pearl Resorts provides an unrivaled haven of peace and quiet with its stunning background of blue seas and white sand beaches.

Elevated at the top of a hill overlooking Maputo Bay, the Cardoso Hotel is a tribute to classic elegance. It is a sanctuary for anyone looking for a sophisticated getaway because of its exquisite accommodations, attentive service, and atmosphere of understated elegance. The combination of Portuguese and Mozambican influences gives the whole experience an additional degree of cultural depth.

The Southern Sun Hotel, located in the center of Maputo, enthralls with its unique mix of contemporary elegance and regional charm. Experience the lively atmosphere of the city while luxuriating in the luxurious lodging and top-notch facilities that this company has to offer. It's an immersion into Mozambique's cultural fabric, not simply a visit.

These opulent lodging options in Maputo, each with its own distinct charm and personality, satisfy even the pickiest tourists and provide a lavish and unforgettable stay in this alluring African city.

Affordable Accommodations

Maputo also provides a selection of reasonably priced lodging options so that visitors may take in all of its attractions without going over budget. The Resotel, which is well located in the center of the city, is an exceptional choice. With spotless rooms and a cozy ambiance, this lodging offers tourists on a tight budget a cozy and reasonably priced sanctuary.

An excellent option for visitors looking for a hotel that combines price and convenience is the Montebelo Indy Maputo Congress Hotel. Its affordable rates and convenient location make it a desirable choice for those who want to see Maputo's highlights without sacrificing accessibility.

Another hidden treasure for travelers on a tight budget is the Hotel Atlantis, which is tucked away in the heart of the city. This lodging takes a no-frills approach to hospitality, making it affordable without sacrificing necessary facilities. This is where cost and usefulness are prioritized above comfort.

For those seeking a more authentic experience, guesthouses like Catembe Gallery Hotel can be of interest. This inexpensive choice, which is located in Catembe across Maputo Bay, offers both affordability and a distinctive view of the town. A guesthouse's unique touch makes the stay seem more cozy.

Furthermore, the Hotel Mozguest, which is centrally situated in downtown Maputo, is a notable example of a budget option without sacrificing comfort. Its modestly styled rooms meet the utilitarian demands of low-budget visitors and provide a handy starting point for seeing the city's many attractions.

Budget accommodations in Maputo are more than just affordable; they're a doorway to the real Maputo without breaking the bank. With these lodging options, visitors may stay within their means and yet experience the warmth and lively culture that characterize this Mozambican city.

Bed and breakfasts and guesthouses

Maputo provides a variety of guesthouses and bed & breakfasts that offer a more individualized and intimate hotel experience, all of which are complemented by the city's warm and eclectic ambiance. At the edge of the city, overlooking Maputo Bay, lies the Catembe Gallery Hotel, which attests to its allure. This guesthouse creates an ambiance that seems like a home away from home by offering comfortable lodging in addition to a distinctive perspective of the metropolis.

Fatima's Backpackers is a well-liked option for travelers looking for a welcoming and social setting in the center of Maputo. In addition to providing reasonably priced lodging, this bed and breakfast encourages a feeling of camaraderie among visitors. Like-minded people may interact and exchange experiences at this center for shared spaces and activities.

Go a little further, and you'll find the Moringa Guest House, a peaceful haven in the middle of the city's bustle. This little guesthouse offers visitors a comfortable haven that blends comfort with a dash of true local flavor. For those who value a more intimate accommodation experience, it stands out for its individualized care and friendly welcome.

The Villa das Mangas Guesthouse, located in the center of the city, provides a window into Maputo's architectural history for those seeking a hint of ancient appeal. With its well-appointed rooms and garden oasis, this hotel from the colonial period offers a tranquil haven in the middle of the busy city.

In addition to being reasonably priced, Maputo's guesthouses and bed & breakfasts are charming because of the unique touch they provide to visitors' trip experiences. For visitors looking for a more personal stay in this fascinating Mozambican city, these lodgings become more than just a place to sleep; they become essential components of the trip experience, crafting a story of connection and local immersion.

Chapter 4

Exploring Maputo Neighborhoods

Exploring Maputo City Center

Located in the center of Maputo, Maputo City Center is a bustling hub that perfectly captures the historical and cultural diversity of Mozambique's capital city. You'll see a distinctive fusion of colonial architecture, cutting-edge infrastructure, and the vibrant local spirit as you make your way through its busy streets.

The city center, which offers a wide range of attractions and activities, acts as a hub for both residents and tourists. Surrounded by important structures like the City Hall and the Maputo Central Market, the renowned Independence Square serves as a tribute to Mozambique's march towards independence. In addition to being a historical landmark, the square serves as a venue for festivals and events that capture the vibrant spirit of Maputo.

You'll come across a variety of modern stores, traditional markets, and restaurants offering real Mozambican food as you meander around the streets. The perfume of freshly made treats fills the air, tempting onlookers to savor the best that Maputo City Center has to offer in terms of cuisine.

The street art and small galleries that line the city's walls, exhibiting the imagination and passion of Mozambican artists, will enthrall art fans. The artwork's striking hues and emotional themes blend perfectly with Maputo's metropolitan landscape's general ambience.

The city center comes alive with a vibrant nightlife scene in the evening. There's a spot for everyone to relax and feel the warmth of Mozambican hospitality, from quiet cafés to bustling pubs. Live music fills the streets with infectious sounds that entice both residents and tourists to partake in the celebrations.

Maputo City Center is more than simply a place; it's a dynamic, living phenomenon that captures the tenacity, variety, and depth of Maputo's culture. This core area captures the essence of the capital city and invites you to become part of its story, whether you're wandering around the old streets, tasting the regional cuisine, or interacting with the lively community.

Polana Area

Maputo, Mozambique's charming Polana area, emanates refinement and old-world charm. Polana, tucked away along the Indian Ocean coast, is a unique jewel in Maputo's colorful mosaic, embodying a fusion of colonial grace and modern charm.

The recognizable Polana Serena Hotel, a representation of classic elegance, is located in the center of Polana. This stately home, with its beautiful grounds and colonial architecture, is a living reminder of the city's illustrious history, in addition to providing luxurious lodging. The hotel has seen much of Mozambique's past, and the echoes of bygone centuries may be heard echoing through its hallways.

Strolling down Polana's tree-lined streets will reveal a community that skillfully blends contemporary and traditional elements. Mansions from the colonial period line the lush alleys; some have been lovingly restored, while others have embraced modernization. The distinct narratives told by each building add to Polana's varied appeal.

Both residents and tourists with sophisticated preferences are catered to by the dynamic Polana Shopping Center. The area's shopping scene, which ranges from elegant boutiques to charming handmade stores, demonstrates how diverse the neighborhood is. Restaurants and cafés provide a great gastronomic experience, allowing patrons to enjoy both local and foreign delicacies in an elegant setting.

Polana's closeness to the Indian Ocean adds to its charm; immaculate beaches entice locals and visitors to take in the sun and explore the turquoise seas. Palm trees cover the shore, offering a peaceful haven in the middle of the busy metropolis. Polana is a sanctuary for those looking to strike a balance between urban elegance and natural peace because of the tranquilizing effect of the sea air.

Polana becomes a lovely sanctuary when the sun sets over the Indian Ocean. The streets are softly lit by streetlights, and quaint taverns and seaside venues are filled with the sound of live music. Polana's nighttime ambience is just amazing, beckoning locals and guests to relish the enchanted moments that make Polana in Maputo an alluring location.

Polana is really more than just a neighborhood; it's a dynamic representation of Maputo's past, a picture that skillfully combines elements of the past and present. Polana presents itself as an engrossing chapter in the story of Maputo's architectural and cultural diversity, whether you want to explore its ancient sites, indulge in its delectable cuisine, or just meander along its charming streets.

Sommerschield

Maputo, Mozambique's Sommerschield neighborhood, is a classy neighborhood that provides a special fusion of refinement, peace, and a distinct cultural atmosphere. This private refuge, tucked away from the busy city center, is distinguished as a sought-after enclave in the capital city by its tree-lined lanes, exquisite residences, and tranquil ambiance.

You will be struck by Sommerschield's subtle beauty and air of exclusivity as you stroll through its verdant streets. Because it is home to a mix of wealthy Mozambican families, expatriate mansions, and diplomatic residences, this area has come to be associated with elite life. A timeless and contemporary look is created by the harmonic fusion of modern and colonial elements in the building.

The Maputo International School, an establishment that serves the community's educational requirements and adds to the area's multicultural vibe, is one of Sommerschield's most noteworthy monuments. International schools provide Sommerschield with a lively new dimension and promote a multicultural and multiethnic community.

The attractiveness of Sommerschield is not limited to its residential aspect. Many high-end businesses, such as boutique stores, fine dining restaurants, and quaint cafés, can be found in the area. These establishments serve the affluent tastes of the neighborhood by offering areas for people to relax, mingle, and savor life's better pleasures.

Sommerschield's closeness to Maputo Bay, which provides breathtaking waterfront views and chances for leisurely strolls along the shoreline, adds to the area's peacefulness. Inside the gates of this exclusive area, the sea wind provides a cool element and a feeling of escape.

Sommerschield assumes a new persona in the evening. The gentle glow of lighting illuminates the streets, fostering a calm and safe atmosphere. Whether you're having a nice dinner at a neighborhood restaurant or just taking a leisurely evening stroll in this tranquil area of Maputo, the environment is ideal for casual interaction.

Sommerschield is a prime example of Maputo's ability to provide a varied quality of life, combining residential refinement, cultural variety, and scenic beauty. This area embodies the growing character of Mozambique's capital city, where tradition and modernity blend to create a unique tapestry.

District of Baixa

The lively neighborhood of Baixa, located in the center of Maputo, Mozambique, throbs with the lively cadence of city life. Baixa, with its vibrant blend of colonial and contemporary architecture, is a tribute to Maputo's tenacity and spirit of adventure.

The vibrant streets of Baixa will engulf you in a kaleidoscope of sights and noises as you walk through them. Mozambique's colonial heritage is reflected in its architecture, which consists of imposing structures with elaborate facades that evoke memories of a bygone period. The juxtaposition with modern architecture draws attention to the city's development and produces an engrossing visual story.

The major avenue of Baixa, Independence Avenue, is the vibrant hub of Maputo's business and cultural life. This lively boulevard, which is lined with government offices, cafés, and stores, is a microcosm of the spirit of the city. The bustling walkways are used by both residents and tourists to create a vibrant atmosphere that embodies Baixa's urban identity.

In addition to being a transit hub and a historical relic, the Central Railway Station is an architectural marvel located in the center of Baixa. Its recognizable iron structure serves as a reminder of Maputo's industrial heritage and provides insight into the evolution of the city throughout time. Maputo City Hall is located nearby and contributes to the district's sense of community by bringing a touch of grandeur to the urban environment.

With the busy Central Market in its center, Baixa is a center of trade as well. The fragrances of fresh fruit, spices, and regional specialties permeate the air here. The market is a sensory feast, with colorful kiosks showcasing the varied gastronomic delights that represent the diversity of Mozambican culture.

Baixa changes after the sun goes down. The streets are lit up by city lights, and the lively nightlife comes to life. For those looking to have fun and mingle, Baixa has a variety of places to choose from, including hip pubs and exciting clubs. Theaters and art galleries contribute to the district's thriving cultural life and its status as a cultural hotspot.

The vibrant fusion of history, business, and culture that is Baixa captures the essence of Maputo. This neighborhood offers an urban setting that encourages investigation and appreciation of Mozambique's rich and varied identity. It is where the past and present collide.

Chapter 5

Top Attractions in Maputo

The Central Market of Maputo

Located in the center of Maputo, the Central Market is a thriving center of trade and culture. Your senses are filled with a kaleidoscope of sights, sounds, and fragrances as you navigate through its busy lanes. The market is a treasure trove of experiences waiting to be discovered and a monument to Maputo's rich history and varied cultures.

A dizzying selection of fresh goods, from luscious, sun-kissed fruits to a variety of locally produced veggies, fills the stalls. Vendors call with smiles and lively discussions, giving not just items but also a look into the warmth of Mozambican hospitality. Each vendor has a story woven into the fabric of the market.

As you get further, the air fills with the rich aroma of spices—a harmonious blend of cardamom, cloves, and coriander that creates a sensory tour of Mozambique's culinary customs. Here, the skill of negotiating takes on the qualities of a cultural dance, a rhythmic conversation, and laughter that go beyond simple business dealings.

More than just a market, the Central Market is a live gallery where craftspeople display their skills via elaborate wood carvings, colorful textiles, and traditional items. Every component weaves together the strands of the country's history and customs to convey a tale.

The architecture of the market is a reminder of a bygone age among the colorful pandemonium. The wrought-iron accents and arched doors, which contrast with the modern vitality, are clear reminders of colonial influence. It's an area where the past and present come together to weave a unique tapestry that characterizes Maputo.

The market's vibrant energy is accompanied by the rhythmic rhythms of local music that permeate the air. Both locals and tourists explore the maze-like hallways, finding hidden treasures and creating relationships that cut across linguistic boundaries.

The market changes throughout the course of the day. You may take your time and enjoy the experience as the hectic morning gives way to a more relaxed pace. Stop by one of the charming restaurants in the market to enjoy some locally sourced cuisine or a freshly made cup of coffee. The unique atmosphere and tastes of the food blend well.

Maputo Central Market is a sensory adventure that offers more than just shopping and selling; there's a tale to be discovered around every turn. It is a microcosm of Maputo itself, full of life, diversity, and the spirit of Mozambique.

Fort Maputo (Fortaleza)

Fortaleza, also known as Maputo Fort, is perched magnificently on the shores of Maputo Bay, acting as a quiet watchdog over the passage of time. This ancient site, with its towering stone walls and ageless charm, is proof of the rich history of Maputo and the tenacity of Mozambique's cultural legacy.

Originally built by Portuguese colonial powers as a defensive stronghold against sea attacks, the fort dates back to the late 1700s. Its advantageous position, with a view of the Indian Ocean, provided a stronghold for defending the rights of a more distant past. The building captures the complex dance between foreign influence and indigenous identity, combining local workmanship with European military efficiency.

It's as if the worn stones are whispering stories from the past as you meander around the fort's winding passageways. A panoramic picture of the harbor, where the rhythmic waves whisper stories of bygone ages, may be seen from the battlements lined with cannons. The fort itself seems to be a silent narrator, passing down the tales of commerce, conquests, and Maputo's transformation from a sleepy colonial settlement to a thriving city.

A little museum within the fort's walls reveals the facets of its history. Exhibits and artifacts document the many eras of Mozambique's history, ranging from the early colonial era to the liberation movements. Every exhibit is a stroke on the canvas of time, depicting vividly the struggles endured and victories cherished inside these stone walls.

However, Fortaleza is more than simply a historical artifact—it is a vibrant center of culture. The sounds of traditional music and the laughter of the residents fill the courtyard, which is often the site of events and gatherings. The vibrant contemporary contrast with the historic setting creates an enthralling dance between tradition and advancement.

The atmosphere changes as the sun sets and casts a warm light on the aged face of the fort. Strollers walk along the waterfront promenade in the evening, the dramatic shadow formed by the fort's silhouette. Couples, families, and friends join together to enjoy moments in front of this eternal emblem, transforming the event into a timeless spectacle that is a marriage of the past and present.

Maputo Fort is more than just a historical remnant because of its enduring charm. It is a living example of a country's tenacity, a repository of narratives, and a stage for the symphony of the past and present. Fortaleza's tales and stones beckon tourists to immerse themselves in the captivating tale of

Mozambique's historical journey rather than just observe history.

Maputo Train Station

Situated in the center of Maputo, the Railway Station is more than just a transit center—it is a dynamic example of the interwoven stories of development, culture, and architectural splendor. A feeling of historical importance descends over you as you approach the station, and the repetitive clatter of leaving trains forms the soundtrack to Maputo's lively pulse.

Built in the recognizable Beaux-Arts architectural style of the early 20th century, the station is a massive building with many fine features. The exterior has towering arches and elaborate embellishments that evoke the dreams of a bygone period. It is a tasteful fusion of European grandeur and local elements. It's an artistic symphony that preserves its traditional heritage while encapsulating Mozambique's embrace of modernity.

Entering the station is similar to entering a time capsule. The expansive space emanates a timeless refinement with its polished flooring and towering ceilings. The vast hall of the station, with its antique chandeliers and shiny hardwood chairs, is alive with the sounds of many passengers coming and going. It's a place where the past and present collide, and the air is heavy with the promise of adventures to come.

The platform, a busy roadway, presents a small-scale representation of Maputo's variety. Travelers, residents, and commuters all go across the platform, each with a unique destination and tale to tell. The suppliers,

Maputo Elephant Reserve

The Elephant Reserve is a nature refuge surrounded by urbanity, tucked away on Maputo's outskirts. Nature lovers and thrill seekers alike are drawn to this ecological oasis, which is proof of Mozambique's dedication to conservation. It provides a break from the bustle of the city and a window into its natural beauty.

Excitement mounts as you follow the winding trails that lead into the reserve. The smells of dirt and greenery fill the air, while the sounds of distant bird cries and rustling leaves take the place of the city's orchestra. The reserve is home to a wide range of flora and animals, but the magnificent elephants are the undeniable stars of this amazing natural show. The reserve is a patchwork of varied habitats.

Visitors may see these gentle giants in their native environment during guided safari trips, which are done with a careful balance between respect for the animals and educational knowledge. A strong bond with the natural environment is formed when one spots a family of elephants frolicking in a watering hole or grazing on the golden savannah. It serves as a reminder of how crucial it is to protect these kinds of habitats in order to protect these amazing animals as well as the fragile ecosystems they live in.

The reserve offers a picture of wildlife in addition to elephants. Enthralling and enlightening, the variety of wildlife includes everything from elegant impalas to secretive leopards. The vivid plumage of exotic birds flutters over the vegetation, and birdwatchers are in heaven as their haunting cries reverberate through the air. Every living item on this dynamic, breathing canvas is essential to the complex dance of nature.

The reserve serves as a living school for conservation as well as a refuge for animals. The reserve's educational initiatives and interpretive centers help people learn about the fragile balance of ecosystems and how important it is for humanity to preserve biodiversity. It's a location where consciousness grows, encouraging a feeling of obligation to the environment and the unique animals that live in the Elephant Reserve.

The terrain itself is a contrast study. The environment changes from broad meadows to thick forests like a book, with each chapter showcasing a different aspect of nature's creative expression. With their expansive views and ability to take in the majesty of the reserve and the surrounding landscapes, elevated overlooks provide visitors with a multisensory experience that goes beyond the visual.

A feeling of thankfulness permeates the air as the sun sets over the Elephant Reserve, bathing the grassland in a warm light. Thank you for the chance to see the natural beauty of Maputo's wildness and for your committed efforts to conserve it. The Elephant Reserve, with its magnificent residents and immaculate surroundings, serves as a reminder of our shared duty to protect the planet's priceless inheritance, in addition to serving as a monument to Mozambique's natural treasures.

The Independence Square

The vibrant center of Maputo, Praça da Independência, is a fascinating mosaic of culture, history, and modern life. This large plaza, which is encircled by magnificent buildings, is a vibrant hub where Mozambique's spirit of independence is evident everywhere.

The Monument to Independence, a towering and majestic representation of the country's arduous freedom struggle, sits in the middle of the plaza. The jubilant marching bronze figures depict a spirit of resiliency and solidarity that epitomizes Mozambique's path to independence. It is more than just a sculpture; it is a living representation of the hardships, giving ups, and triumphs that help to form the identity of the country.

With their delicate pastel colors and fine details, the colonial-era buildings that surround the plaza provide an air of vintage charm. Maputo's unique fusion of African and European elements is exemplified by the magnificent City Hall. Its façade, with its elaborate balconies and arched windows, creates a visual link between the city's dynamic present and its colonial history.

Praça da Independência becomes a hive of activity as the day goes on. Both locals and visitors congregate to take in the vibrant atmosphere. A kaleidoscope of colors and tastes is created by the street sellers that line the paths, providing a wide variety of refreshments, crafts, and souvenirs. The colorful picture is enhanced with a musical background as street performers fill the air with their beat.

Restaurants and cafés overflow the area, beckoning customers to enjoy the regional cuisine while observing street life. The square's colorful tapestry of life is best seen from the front row of seats provided by the outdoor seating. It's a place where laughter reverberates, discussions flow easily, and

Maputo's vitality is evident in every move and emotion.

The area takes on a wonderful character when the sun sets. Warm colors surround the Monument to Independence, giving the surrounding buildings a soft light. Now that it is lit, Maputo's City Hall acts as a quiet observer of its changing history.

Praça da Independência is a real, breathing place that captures the essence of Maputo; it is more than simply a location on a map. It's a location where the pulse of the present blends with the echoes of the past, fostering an atmosphere that celebrates freedom in all its forms, historical and modern.

Chapter 6

Cultural Experiences in Maputo

Cuisine of Mozambique

Maputo's Mozambican cuisine is a complex tapestry of tastes that draws on the nation's close proximity to the Indian Ocean and rich cultural variety. The

Portuguese colonial past has left a lasting impression on Maputo's culinary scene, fusing well-known African products and cooking methods.

It is impossible to explore Mozambican food without tasting the famous peri-peri sauce. This hot sauce, made from the powerful African bird's eye chili, gives a lot of different foods a rush of heat. Street food favorites include grilled chicken marinated in peri-peri sauce, or "frango grelhado," as it is called locally. The air is filled with the inviting scent of grilling, drawing in both residents and tourists.

The culinary scene of Maputo is dominated by seafood. Because of the city's seaside position, fresh catches are consistently available, with prawns, lobster, and a variety of fish kinds being the most popular options. The famous "camarão à la Mozambicana" meal was delicious coconut milk sauce prepared with juicy prawns that give it a creamy, tropical flavor.

The basic elements of Mozambican cuisine are cassava, millet, and maize. The traditional delicacy "Matapa," which is cooked to perfection with crushed peanuts and coconut milk, demonstrates the adaptability of cassava leaves. This tasty mixture is proof of the creativity of Mozambican chefs, who turn common items into mouthwatering creations.

Explore a kaleidoscope of colors and scents at Maputo's busy marketplaces. Tropical fruit stands with colorful mounds of mangoes, papayas, and bananas entice, while spice shops provide a variety of mouthwatering concoctions. The "Mercado Central," or central market, is a bustling meeting place where both residents and visitors share ideas on fresh produce, spices, and cooking techniques.

Eating in Maputo is an immersion in culture as well as a culinary adventure. Sharing meals with others is a social practice that embodies the warmth and friendliness that characterize Mozambican culture. Every mouthful of food, whether it's grilled seafood on the beach, traditional stews, or dishes laced with peri-peri, tells a tale about the history, geography, and tenacity of the people of Mozambique. The food scene of Maputo welcomes you to join them on a savory trip where each dish celebrates Mozambican culture and the distinctive fusion of influences that characterize this alluring cuisine.

Customary Dance and Music

Maputo's traditional dance and music are more than simply artistic creations; they are dynamic representations of Mozambique's rich and varied cultural heritage. These historically significant performances are a colorful tapestry woven with the strands of custom, religion, and communal joy.

Maputo's indigenous music has a tempo that reflects the pulse of the country. Inspired by a synthesis of Portuguese, Bantu, and Swahili cultural influences, the music is a soulful combination of unique fusions. The xylophone, marimba, and drums are prominent traditional instruments that create songs that depict the region, its people, and their common experiences.

Maputo's traditional music scene would be incomplete without experiencing the timbila's captivating tones. Crafted from gourd resonators and wooden slats, this xylophone-like instrument creates complex melodies that take listeners to the core of Mozambique's cultural legacy. Timbila orchestras are a monument to the skill and talent ingrained in traditional Mozambican music, with their throbbing rhythms and mellow melodies.

Maputo's musical legacy is not complete without dance, which is a vibrant way to convey feelings, customs, and group identity. Traditional dances are often performed at ceremonial occasions, during rites of passage, or to mark noteworthy occasions. The "Makwayela" dance is an enthralling demonstration of storytelling via movement, distinguished by its rhythmic feet and expressive gestures. Vibrantly dressed dancers provide a visual spectacle that reflects the vitality of Mozambican culture.

In Maputo, dance and music permeate daily life and are not limited to formal performances or stages. Markets, festivals, and get-togethers turn into spontaneous events when the upbeat steps and steady rhythms of traditional dance fill the air with enthusiasm and vitality. It's a multigenerational event that fosters pride in Mozambique's cultural past and a feeling of continuity.

In spiritual rituals and ceremonies, traditional dance and music are equally essential. Rituals that include symbolic dances and drumming beats foster a sense of community and ancestry among participants. The way the festive and the holy are entwined highlights how comprehensive Maputo's traditional creative manifestations are.

Traditional dance and music continue to serve as cultural pillars in Maputo, keeping the populace grounded while also offering a stage for creative expression. Tradition and new expression coexist in a vibrant cultural environment created by the juxtaposition of antiquated rhythms with current inspirations. Traditional dance and music in Maputo are living traditions that reflect the soulful pulse of Mozambique's cultural identity. They are not only performances.

Markets for Arts and Crafts

Maputo's arts and crafts markets provide a fascinating window into Mozambique's dynamic cultural environment, weaving a vivid tapestry of creativity and tradition. Located all across the city, these vibrant markets are true treasure troves where regional craftspeople display their talents and guests are treated to a sensory extravaganza of handcrafted marvels.

As you go through the markets, you can't help but be amazed by the rainbow of colors that cover the shops and kiosks. Beaded jewelry, vivid fabrics, and intricately woven baskets combine to create a visual symphony that represents the variety of influences influencing Mozambican craftsmanship. Every piece combines history and modern design to convey a tale that is often based on centuries-old methods that have been handed down through the generations.

The focus on traditional craftsmanship is one of these marketplaces' most notable characteristics. Expert craftspeople, who are often members of the local community, painstakingly produce objects that reflect Mozambique's rich cultural past. The sound of traditional fabric loom weaving, like the famous capulana, fills the air with a rhythmic clatter that enhances the immersive shopping experience.

Mozambican artists' skill is shown by their expertise in woodcarving. Crafted from native woods, exquisite sculptures and elaborate masks display the artistry of the artisans as well as the cultural importance inherent in each creation. Whether they represent animals or ancestors, these sculptures provide concrete connections to Mozambique's customs and culture.

Looking around the marketplaces for arts and crafts is like taking a cultural tour. Every market has its own distinct appeal, from the colorful booths of the FEIMA Artisanal Market to the varied choices of Mercado Central. Discover handcrafted musical instruments, leather products, and ceramics that showcase the variety of Mozambican artistry.

Maputo's markets provide a chance to interact with the craftspeople directly in addition to purchasing real goods. Speaking with these gifted people reveals the pride and passion they bring to their job. Understanding the origins of each piece's designs, their cultural relevance, and the creative processes involved improves one's enjoyment of the artwork on exhibit.

In addition to being places for commerce, the arts and crafts fairs serve as foci for cross-cultural interaction. By interacting with the residents, visitors may learn more about their way of life and the tales that are weaved into their artwork. It's a combination of business and cultural immersion, where each purchase serves as a significant link to the creative legacy of Mozambique.

There is a noticeable blend of innovation and heritage in the middle of the busy marketplaces. Old methods and contemporary versions of traditional crafts coexist, demonstrating the versatility and vibrancy of Mozambique's creative community. Maputo's arts and crafts markets are more than just places to buy; they're living galleries honoring the inventiveness, variety, and resilient spirit of Mozambican innovation.

Events and Festivals of Culture

During its colorful festivals and cultural events, Maputo, the beating heart of Mozambique, comes alive with a kaleidoscope of colors, rhythms, and customs. These festivities are more than simply events; they are a representation of the many cultures that make up the country and a chance for the city to come alive with joy, creativity, and the preservation of history.

An incredible display of traditional dance and song, the Mapiko Festival, is proof of Mozambique's dedication to maintaining its cultural heritage. This event, which takes place every year, features the well-known Mapiko dance, in which dancers wear intricate masks and costumes and use rhythmic movements to narrate tales of community, spirituality, and history. It's a captivating show that goes beyond amusement and offers a strong link to Mozambique's ancient customs.

The Marrabenta Festival makes Maputo's streets come alive with the sound of traditional drums filling the air. Mozambique's musical skill is shown by this celebration of Marrabenta, the nation's hallmark musical style. It's a time when regional and foreign musicians come together to celebrate the variety of sounds—from lively rhythms to heartfelt melodies—that characterize Mozambican identity.

Maputo's Carnaval is a spectacular celebration of color and vivacity that perfectly embodies the festive atmosphere. The city is turned into a vibrant carnival with costumes, floats, and processions. The contagious sounds of samba and traditional Mozambican music fill the streets, drawing people from all walks of life to experience the festive mood. It's an event that breaks down barriers by bringing residents and guests together for a common good time.

Maputo's standing as a center of culture is further cemented by the AZGO Festival, a mash-up of arts and culture. Every year, performers, poets, visual artists, and musicians from Mozambique and beyond come together for this occasion. The festival's varied schedule promotes artistic interchange and a feeling of intercultural harmony, including music performances, visual art displays, and thought-provoking talks.

Maputo organizes several cultural events all year long that honor the variety of languages spoken in the nation. Poets from Mozambique and other countries participate in the Festival Internacional de Poesia, which honors the expressive power of poetry. The Maputo International Film Festival gives filmmakers an opportunity to tell their tales while showcasing artistic works that capture the social fiber of the country.

Maputo's festivals often include customary rites and ceremonies in addition to cultural pursuits. Timbila, the traditional music played on the xylophone by the Chopi, is celebrated together with cultural events, resulting in a harmonic fusion of traditional and modern emotions.

Attending these celebrations and cultural activities is an invitation to fully immerse oneself in Maputo culture, not only to observe. The city's celebrations provide a strong link to the past, resilience, and spirit of Mozambique's people. The melodies that fill music halls and the beat of traditional dances are just two examples of how Maputo's cultural events celebrate life, variety, and the eternal power of creative expression.

Chapter 7

Outdoor Activities in Maputo

Beaches and water sports in Maputo

Mozambique's main city, Maputo, is home to breathtaking beaches along its coastline. Maputo Beach, a tranquil length of golden sand lapped by the Indian Ocean, is one such beauty. The beach provides the ideal getaway because of the peaceful ambiance created by the warm sun and steady waves.

Maputo Beach is a sanctuary for those who love water activities. The alternatives are many, ranging from thrilling jet skiing to more relaxed paddleboarding. The lively underwater world is revealed by snorkeling in the crystal-clear waters, which provide for a perfect location.

Diving options abound, enabling you to explore coral reefs teaming with marine life for those looking for a more immersive experience. Beginner surfers looking to catch their first wave will also find the beach to be a great place to ride the mild waves.

The beach is a place to relax as well as engage in exciting water sports. Imagine yourself walking down the beach, the powdery sand under your feet, watching as the sun dips below the horizon, casting orange and pink streaks across the sky.

Locals often set up shop along the shore to sell delectable fish and cool drinks. The Maputo Beach experience is completed by savoring a seafood feast or a fresh coconut while listening to the sound of the ocean.

In conclusion, Maputo's beaches provide a perfect balance of leisure and exploration, making them an essential destination for anybody wishing to appreciate the splendor of Mozambique's coastal landscapes.

Special Reserve of Maputo

Tucked away along Mozambique's southern coast, the Maputo Special Reserve is a little-known treasure that demonstrates how committed the nation is to protecting its natural beauties. This exceptional sanctuary is a playground for nature lovers and a refuge for animals, showcasing a mosaic of varied habitats, from vast marshes to immaculate coastal dunes.

As soon as one sets out into the center of the reserve, they are astounded by the enormous variety of plants and animals that make this refuge home. Elevated sand woodlands transition to expansive savannahs, where antelopes amble with elegance, and marshlands are brimming with birds, producing a cacophonous chorus of vocalizations that fill the atmosphere.

The estuary system, where the waters of the Maputo River meet the Indian Ocean, is one of the reserve's main attractions. Numerous bird species seek shelter in the tangle of branches, and mangrove-lined waterways weave across the terrain, creating a flourishing ecology where crocodiles and hippos lurk under the surface.

Guided walking safaris provide an immersive experience of the sights and sounds of the reserve for those who are looking for a more personal relationship with nature. Discover the mysteries of the bush with knowledgeable guides who point out animal traces and tell stories about the intricate web of life that exists in this natural preserve.

The reserve's expansive coastline, with its unspoiled beaches and crystal-clear seas, provides a peaceful haven. Imagine yourself enjoying the unspoiled beauty of the Mozambican coastline while relaxing on the beach with the soothing sound of the waves in the background.

The main goal of the Maputo Special Reserve is conservation. Devoted endeavors guarantee the preservation of threatened species, and continuous investigation advances our comprehension of the intricate equilibrium present in this environment. It is a living laboratory where the subtleties of nature are appreciated and examined.

The Maputo Special Reserve, which invites everyone to enter its embrace and experience the raw beauty of Mozambique's southern border, is really more than just a wildlife reserve. It is a living, breathing example of the symbiotic interaction between man and nature.

Chapter 8

Shopping/Purchasing in Maputo

Regional souks and markets

Maputo is home to a plethora of vivid local marketplaces and souks that are a riot of color and energy. Moving through these busy centers is a sensory experience, with the fragrances of far-off spices blending with the brilliant colors of fresh vegetables.

Maputo cannot be fully experienced without spending time at the local markets, which are the beating heart of the city. The Central Market offers a wide variety of products, from handmade textiles to fragrant herbs, all tucked away in its maze-like alleyways. Interacting with the local sellers exposes a thriving community as well as a marketplace, with each booth serving as a representation of Maputo's artisanal pride.

The night market comes to life as the sun sets, illuminating the city with a mystical hue. Street food is sizzling all around, from fragrant skewers of spicy peri-peri chicken to luscious grilled prawns. It's a gastronomic experience that goes beyond simple nourishment, beckoning guests to revel in the spirit of Mozambican cuisine.

When strolling around Baixa's Souk, one comes across an abundance of traditional antiquities and handcrafted goods. From bright paintings depicting the nation's illustrious past to elaborately woven baskets, the artwork on show illustrates the cultural richness of Mozambique. Every object narrates a tale that is interwoven with Maputo's national identity.

The market experience is more than just shopping; it's a celebration of custom and community. Local musicians create a soothing atmosphere by combining their beats with the background noise of giggling and haggling. The fusion of trade and culture produces a mood that is unique to Maputo.

Haggling is an art form as well as a necessary transaction in these marketplaces. It's a verbal and facial dance, a social interaction that connects the buyer and seller. These discussions provide one with a memento as well as an insight into the kindness and tenacity of the Maputo people.

In the end, Maputo's neighborhood markets and souks represent the spirit of the city and go beyond the transactional aspect of trade. These are places where the lively symphony of Maputo's marketplaces is alive with activity, where the heartbeat of everyday life beats in unison with the city's rich cultural legacy.

Contemporary Shopping Malls

Maputo welcomes the contemporary age with a variety of state-of-the-art shopping malls that are redefining the city's retail experience in its constantly changing urban environment. These modern hubs give a window into Maputo's multicultural ethos by skillfully fusing international styles with a unique Mozambican flair.

The Polana retail center is one of the most elegant contemporary retail locations in the city. Its modern architecture and posh stores provide a carefully chosen shopping experience where local designers and global fashion labels mix to create a vibrant mixture of trends. The elegant atmosphere provides a haven of luxury and sophistication away from the busy streets.

The Maputo Shopping Center is an expansive complex that offers a wide range of options for anyone looking for a thorough shopping experience. This shopping destination is the definition of convenience, with everything from upscale clothing stores to electronics shops and fine dining establishments. Its wide hallways entice guests to explore, with each retailer revealing a hidden gem of modern merchandise.

The entertainment component of shopping is enhanced by the existence of contemporary movie theaters in these malls. Indulge in the newest film options, resulting in a smooth fusion of retail therapy and relaxation. The air is filled with the perfume of freshly made coffee from hip cafés, giving customers a break from their explorations and a chance to refresh.

In the Maputo Technology Park, where state-of-the-art devices and inventions take center stage, tech aficionados find comfort. This futuristic retail location appeals to tech-savvy consumers by providing a peek at the newest developments and fostering an immersive atmosphere that piques interest and enthusiasm.

These contemporary shopping complexes are social hubs where the community congregates, which adds to their appeal beyond retail therapy. Weekend excursions with friends, business meetings, and family get-togethers all take place in these fashionable settings. These areas grow to be essential parts of Maputo's social fabric, promoting relationships among modern materialism.

Essentially, Maputo's contemporary retail complexes are mirrors of the city's changing character rather than only being places for commerce. They represent the fusion of regional quirks and global influences, weaving tradition and modernity together to create a tapestry. Whether one is looking for the newest gadgets, gastronomic adventures, or fashion trends, these retail malls entice everyone to experience the vibrant modernity of Maputo.

Handicrafts and art from Mozambique

The elaborate tapestry of handicrafts and artwork that decorate Maputo's marketplaces and galleries brings Mozambique's creative essence to life. The city is a platform for the colorful manifestations of Mozambican creativity, where modern art and traditional handicraft come together to depict the history of a culturally diverse country.

Discovering the many local marketplaces, such as the Arts and Crafts Market or the Feira Popular, reveals an array of Mozambican handicrafts. Engraved with symbolic designs, wooden carvings are a monument to the deft hands that have crafted things for millennia. These objects embody the spiritual essence of Mozambique's many ethnic groups, in addition to being ornamental pieces.

The capulana, a traditional Mozambican cloth that tells stories of identity and history, is irresistible. This beautiful textile, which is often used to make apparel and home goods, depicts the rich cultural diversity of the nation. The marketplaces are a veritable gold mine of Capulana handicrafts, ranging from elaborately crafted accessories to apparel, each item bearing a story that links to Mozambique's history and present.

Visiting the many art galleries located in Maputo reveals a modern viewpoint on the creativity of Mozambique. Both recognized and up-and-coming local artists utilize their canvases to explore a variety of issues, from environmental concern to social justice. The fusion of avant-garde ideas and conventional methods produces a vibrant art scene that reflects the nation's dynamic character.

One example of Mozambique's dedication to promoting creative expression is the well-known Núcleo de Arte in Maputo. A wide range of media, including paintings and sculptures, are on display here, with each work adding to the lively cultural conversation. The exhibition acts as a conversation starter, bringing together artists and art lovers to appreciate Mozambique's distinctive visual language.

Another aspect of the regional cultural tapestry is Mozambican beading, in which little beads are combined to create elaborate designs that convey spiritual and traditional tales. In addition to displaying the fine workmanship, necklaces, bracelets, and other beaded items serve as physical reminders of Mozambique's rich cultural history.

These creative creations represent the inventiveness and resiliency of a country that has triumphed over hardship, going beyond simple beauty. Maputo is transformed into a live gallery via handicrafts and artwork, allowing tourists to fully experience the visual symphony of Mozambican culture. Throughout the voyage, each brushstroke, carved detail, and bead woven into elaborate patterns serves as a window into the spirit of a country whose artists help it find its voice.

Chapter 9

Dining and Cuisine in Maputo

Street food and dishes from Mozambique

Discovering Maputo's Mozambican cuisine is a colorful trip through a tapestry of tastes that captures the nation's many cultural influences. Maputo, the nation's capital, has a cosmopolitan food culture that combines native foods with Portuguese, Indian, and Arab flavors.

"Matapa," a traditional meal prepared of cassava leaves, crushed peanuts, coconut milk, and a variety of spices, is a great place to start your culinary journey. Its unique flavor and creamy texture highlight the blending of Portuguese and indigenous cooking traditions.

The smell of "Piri Piri" chicken permeates the air as you make your way through the busy streets. Mozambique's Afro-Portuguese ancestry is embodied in this spicy treat, marinated in a hot combination of chili peppers, garlic, and lemon. For a really genuine taste, pair it with "Pozinho," a bread inspired by Portuguese cuisine.

Don't miss Maputo's many delicious street food options. "Chamussas," which are similar to Indian samosas, are aromatic pastry stuffed with meat or veggies and make a delicious snack while you explore the bustling marketplaces.

For those who love seafood, the seashore flavor is evident in meals like "Matapa de Peixe," which is a fish take on the classic matapa, or the famous "Chamussas de Camarão," which are pastries packed with shrimp that perfectly embody the spirit of Mozambican seaside living.

Discover hidden treasures like "Barraca da Pipa," where you can have "Caril de Galinha," a savory chicken curry mixed with native spices and served with aromatic rice, when you explore the lively street food scene in the Baixa area.

Indulge in "Bolo Polana," a coconut and cashew cake that perfectly captures the tropical aromas of Mozambique, to satisfy your sweet craving. "Ginguba," a peanut brittle that is often sold at street stands, will provide a crunchy end to your culinary adventure.

Every meal in Maputo reflects the fusion of several cultures, offering gastronomic enthusiasts a unique and remarkable experience. Maputo's Mozambican cuisine allows you to experience the essence of the country, one delicious taste at a time, from the bustling street markets to the charming restaurants.

Best restaurants and Culinary Destinations

Mozambique's capital city, Maputo, entices gourmets with an eclectic mix of fine dining establishments that fuse regional specialties with global inspirations. "Zambi," an elegant restaurant that embodies the spirit of Mozambican food with a contemporary flare, is one particularly noteworthy location. Fresh seafood, such as savory fish and juicy prawns, is featured on this menu. The meal is cooked with a mix of spices that dance on the tongue.

"Avenida" is a great option for those looking for a more personal dining experience because of its attractive environment and food, which artfully blends Mozambican and Portuguese culinary traditions. Every meal, from flavorful soups to grilled meats, narrates the tale of the nation's historical turning points.

Located in the center of Maputo, "Restaurante Costa do Sol" offers a picturesque beachside location. This legendary restaurant, which is well-known for its expansive views and seafood delicacies, welcomes guests to enjoy the sea air while indulging in meals like grilled lobster and calamari, making for a memorable meal by the sea.

The elegant "Varanda Restaurant," located in the lively Polana Serena Hotel, is a gastronomic treasure that brings together local and international delicacies. This restaurant, which offers both international and Mozambican delicacies, is the pinnacle of gastronomic expertise set against an opulent and sophisticated setting.

For those looking for a more laid-back but no less enjoyable experience, the "Feira Popular" market is a hive of activity with an abundance of food booths selling a wide variety of treats. This vibrant market, which offers everything from delicious curries to skewered meats, is a tribute to Maputo's vibrant street food scene.

At "Sundown Sunset Lounge," which is situated on a rooftop with expansive city views, go on a culinary adventure. This chic location is the ideal combination of gastronomic pleasure and social atmosphere, serving as a destination for evening drinks in addition to providing a delicious meal.

"Piri-Piri" is a neighborhood favorite that stands out in the center of Baixa. Known for its hot peri-peri chicken, this little restaurant embodies the spirit of street cuisine in Mozambique with its robust tastes and relaxed vibe.

Maputo's gastronomic landscape entices discovery, creating a tapestry of tastes that honors the nation's ethnic variety and rich past. Whether you choose upscale restaurants, beachfront hideaways, or vibrant marketplaces, every Maputo culinary destination enhances the city's standing as a food lover's paradise.

Choices for International Cuisine

The dynamic city of Mozambique, Maputo, welcomes variety in its food scene and provides a wide range of foreign dining alternatives to suit a global palette. "Mundo's" stands out as a top option for anyone who is hankering for the mouthwatering tastes of the Mediterranean. This restaurant, which offers Greek salads, Italian pastas, and Spanish paellas, is tucked away in the center of Maputo and offers a taste of the Mediterranean there.

With its variety of Asian delicacies, "Nthalire Restaurant" welcomes you if your gastronomic adventure takes you to the Far East. With dishes ranging from sushi rolls to Thai curries, this restaurant expertly embodies Asian cuisine. The traditional food and the exquisite environment combine to provide a dining experience that goes beyond national boundaries.

For those who like French food, "La Bonne Table" is a monument to skill in the kitchen. This little café serves traditional French cuisine that is well prepared with style. From coq au vin to escargot, every dish takes guests to the heart of France while retaining a uniquely Maputo flair.

The blending of South American and African elements is seen in "Casa Elefante." This diverse restaurant offers a cuisine that combines Brazilian and Mozambican tastes, and it has a lively ambiance and colorful décor. Anticipate fare like feijoada and piri-piri-infused treats that highlight the fusion of cultures across continents.

"Annapurna" exposes Maputo to the colorful world of Indian food for a taste of the unusual. This restaurant offers a sensory voyage through the spices and textures of the subcontinent, bringing the tastes of India to the coasts of Mozambique. Dishes include creamy curries and fragrant biryanis.

Maputo's foreign fusion restaurants, like "Tamarind," showcase its cosmopolitan flare by blurring culinary borders to create meals that expertly combine inspirations from throughout the world. Diners are invited to go on a gastronomic voyage at this cutting-edge restaurant, experiencing meals that are inspired by different parts of the globe.

Discover restaurants like "Sitar," which serves genuine Middle Eastern food, and "Milano," an Italian paradise where pizza and pasta are made with love, as you explore Maputo's culinary scene. These selections highlight the city's dedication to offering a wide range of foreign cuisines, guaranteeing that Maputo's rich and varied culinary tapestry will satisfy any palate.

Chapter 10

Maputo's Nightlife and Entertainment

Nightclubs and bars

Maputo is home to a thriving nightlife culture that offers both residents and tourists a wide range of experiences in its pubs and clubs. The city comes alive with the vibrant ambiance and rhythmic rhythms of its nightlife as the sun sets over the Indian Ocean.

The Polana Bar, located within the storied Polana Serena Hotel, is one famous location. This elegant location offers the ideal ambiance for a more laid-back evening by blending traditional charm with contemporary flare. A classic Maputo experience is sipping on a unique drink while taking in the expansive vistas of the city lights.

It is essential to visit the Feira Popular de Maputo if you're looking for a livelier atmosphere. After nightfall, this expansive fairground becomes a hive of activity, with a wide variety of pubs and clubs to suit all interests. The vibrant lights, lively throng, and pounding music combine to create an exuberant environment that perfectly captures Maputo's evening.

Located in the center of the city, Coconuts Live is a well-liked nightclub that draws visitors as well as residents. This establishment is well-known for its wide range of musical choices, which include worldwide hits and Afro-rhythms. It promises an endless dance night. Those who want to let loose and experience Maputo's nightlife culture love it because of the lively energy of the crowd and the upbeat music.

Scattered over Maputo, the Marrabenta Clubs provide a distinctive experience for anyone seeking a taste of true local life. These venues provide live performances that highlight traditional rhythms in honor of Mozambique's rich musical legacy, especially in the Marrabenta genre. It's an opportunity to take in the music and establish a connection with the city's vibrant cultural scene.

Stumbling upon Maputo's hidden treasures, which are little pubs nestled away in the city's nooks, is possible while strolling around the streets. These less-known places often provide a more intimate and genuine experience, enabling guests to strike up discussions with locals and other tourists and make memories that last long after the night ends.

To sum up, Maputo's pubs and clubs provide a wide range of experiences, from elegant lounges to vibrant dance floors and locations with a strong cultural heritage. Discovering the city's nightlife is an adventure into Maputo's soul, where the lively energy of the populace blends with the beat of the night. It's not only about the cocktails and music, however.

Live music venues

The dynamic pulses of live music venues in Maputo, the beating heart of Mozambique, provide an experience that music lovers cannot have anywhere else. The city's live music industry is a tribute to its vast cultural diversity, ranging from little venues that resound with the heartfelt sounds of local performers to bigger stages that accommodate worldwide stars.

The Gil Vicente Lounge is one notable location; it's a moody area where jazz melodies blend well with Afrobeats' upbeat rhythms. Located in the center of Maputo, this lounge invites guests to fully immerse themselves in the live performances by providing a warm and inviting atmosphere in addition to a varied musical selection.

The Centro Cultural Franco-Moçambicano (CCFM) offers a sample of Mozambique's musical history and is a cultural haven. Live music performances, including traditional genres from the nation, such as Marrabenta and Manganbeu, are held at this versatile venue. For those who like music, the combination of modern sounds with Mozambican heritage offers a genuine and rewarding experience.

The Festa de Mocambique is a street celebration that ventures into the historic quarter and turns Maputo into a massive music arena. With captivating performances that highlight the variety of Mozambique's music landscape, local artists take center stage. For those looking for an immersive musical experience, it's a must-attend event because of the vibrant environment and sense of community.

Nestled in a calm area of the city, the Marrabenta Sol Garden presents a special blend of nature and live music. This modest venue, which is surrounded by beautiful vegetation, presents live concerts and acoustic sessions for both established and up-and-coming musicians. For individuals who value the harmony between music and the natural environment, it's a sanctuary.

The Bar Lounge 1908 is a popular venue that skillfully combines a love of live music with current aesthetics for a more modern feel. This venue's varied program, which includes anything from techno artists to indie bands, draws a wide range of people. For music enthusiasts, the cozy environment and top-notch sound system guarantee an unforgettable experience.

Discovering Maputo's live music scene is an adventure into Mozambique's cultural spirit, not only about the performances. Each location has its own personality that adds to the rich tapestry of sounds that depicts the history, challenges, and victories of the country. Live music venues in Maputo provide an amazing auditory experience, whether you're at a busy street festival or a cozy jazz bar.

Theaters and cultural events

Maputo is a vibrant, culturally rich city that showcases its creative tapestry via theater and cultural events that deeply honor Mozambican tradition and enthrall spectators. These spaces are important for maintaining and advancing the rich cultural character of the country, in addition to showcasing theatrical excellence.

Maputo's dedication to the theatrical arts is shown by the renowned Teatro Avenida, located in the city's center. Numerous shows, from modern musicals to classic plays, are presented at this historic theater. It is a cultural sanctuary for both residents and tourists, with its exquisite architecture and cozy atmosphere serving as the ideal setting for theater productions.

The Centro Cultural Franco-Moçambicano (CCFM) is a vibrant cultural center that offers a combination of traditional and contemporary acts. This center presents dance, music, and visual arts in addition to theater acts. It acts as a melting pot where various creative expressions come together to promote intercultural communication and enhance Maputo's cultural environment.

With its roots in Mozambique's rich musical history, the Marrabenta drama presents a distinctive blend of music and drama. This location presents shows that blend stories with Marrabenta's soul-stirring melodies to create a visceral experience that speaks to the nation's core. It is evidence of how theater develops into a vehicle for using music to arouse feelings in addition to telling tales.

Taking to the streets for the Festa de Mocambique, where Maputo becomes an outdoor theater, This colorful event features dance, street theater, and traditional acts that weave a dynamic tapestry of Mozambican culture along the city's thoroughfares and squares. The Festa de Mocambique is an example of how cultural events use the streets as a platform for public celebration, going beyond traditional theatrical settings.

With its focus on the community, the Maputo Drama League provides theater to the masses. This organization uses theater as a vehicle for social criticism and introspection while interacting with the local populations. Beyond its creative boundaries, theater has the ability to alter; the performances not only amuse but also spark conversation about relevant societal concerns.

Maputo's theaters and cultural events are essentially live representations of Mozambique's vibrant cultural story; they are not limited to the stage. Every location, from the opulence of ancient theaters to the impromptu nature of street shows, adds to a mosaic that showcases the adaptability, inventiveness, and variety of Maputo's cultural landscape. Theater in Maputo is an immersive trip into the essence of a country, whether it's a colorful street performance at a festival or a thought-provoking production at Teatro Avenida.

Chapter 11

Practical Information for Visitors

Travelers' Guide to Safety

Travelers are drawn to Maputo, the energetic capital of Mozambique, by its breathtaking scenery and diverse cultural heritage. Take into account these safety suggestions to guarantee a fun and safe trip:

Study and Strategy: Make it a priority to learn all there is to know about Maputo, including the laws, traditions, and possible hazards. Make sure your plan takes into account popular routes and reliable lodging.

Health Precautions: Before visiting Maputo, get advice from a medical expert about the needed immunizations. Keep a basic medical kit with you, along with any prescription drugs you may need, and know where the nearest hospitals are.

Remain Educated: Stay up to date with current affairs and Mozambique travel advisories. Updates and news from your community might provide important information about any changing circumstances that could affect your safety.

Protect Your Items: Use care while handling personal items. To avoid being pickpocketed, keep your valuables concealed in a pouch or money belt and pay attention to your surroundings. Think about keeping copies of critical papers in a different location.

Transportation Safety: Make sure taxis are legitimate, and choose reliable modes of transportation. Use caution while using public transit, and acquaint yourself with local traffic laws and road conditions if you want to drive.

Cultural Sensitivity: Honor regional traditions and customs. Wear modest clothing, particularly in more traditional settings, and be aware of cultural quirks to promote goodwill among neighbors.

Conversation: To improve conversation, pick up some simple local lingo or carry a translation app. Speaking and understanding the local language may improve your experience and be useful in an emergency.

Stay Out of Dangerous Areas: Know which neighborhoods are more likely to have crimes and stay away from them, particularly after dark. Remain in busy, well-lit locations, and use caution while venturing into uncharted territory.

Contacts for Emergencies: Keep your embassy or consulate's contact details and local emergency numbers handy. Establish frequent check-ins and provide a trustworthy friend or family member access to your schedule.

Insurance for Travel: Invest in comprehensive travel insurance that provides coverage for unexpected events, medical crises, and trip cancellations. Verify Mozambique coverage and familiarize yourself with the policy's terms.

Recall that while enjoying Maputo's natural beauty, a careful and knowledgeable attitude can greatly enhance the likelihood of a safe and enjoyable trip.

Medical and healthcare facilities

Having access to healthcare in Maputo is essential to guaranteeing a fun and safe visit. There are many medical facilities in the city, but it's important to know what to look for when it comes to healthcare and to take the appropriate safety measures.

Overview of Medical Facilities: Maputo is home to several governmental and private hospitals, clinics, and medical facilities. Prominent establishments include Maputo Central Hospital and private establishments such as Clínica Sommerschield. These facilities provide a range of medical services, from regular examinations to emergency treatment.

Healthcare Quality: Although Maputo has respectable hospitals, it's best to have reasonable expectations. Private hospitals often provide a better quality of treatment, but it's important to investigate certain medical facilities and, if at all feasible, get referrals from residents or foreigners.

Language Disparity: Since not everyone speaks English, it might be helpful to know a little bit of

Portuguese or utilize translation applications in order to connect with medical personnel. English-speaking medical personnel are possible, particularly in private clinics that treat patients from other countries.

Medical Insurance: Make getting all-inclusive travel health insurance with emergency medical coverage a top priority. Verify with your insurance company that Maputo is covered, and be aware of the processes for direct billing or reimbursement to nearby hospitals.

Medicines: There are several pharmacies in Maputo where you can get prescription and over-the-counter drugs. Learn where the pharmacies are close to your lodging and make sure you have a basic medical kit with you in case of minor illnesses.

Conditions of Emergency: Dial 117, the local emergency number, in case of an emergency. Prepare yourself to communicate precisely where you are and what kind of emergency it is. For further help, have the contact information for the embassy or consulate of your nation in Maputo handy.

Detailed Attention: It may be required to go to South Africa or other adjacent countries for specialist medical requirements. Make sure that, in the event that medical evacuation is required, your insurance coverage covers this.

Food and Water Safety: Drink bottled or filtered water and watch what you eat—never raw or undercooked—to avoid health problems. Keep an eye on food hygiene procedures to reduce the chance of gastrointestinal ailments.

Preventive Measures: Before departing, get advice from a medical practitioner about the necessary immunizations. Because Mozambique has malaria, talk to your doctor about taking antimalarial drugs and taking the appropriate safety measures to prevent mosquito bites.

Cultural Considerations: Recognize how different cultures view traditional medicine and healthcare. It's possible that local groups follow different customs; acknowledging and appreciating these cultural quirks might improve patient outcomes.

You can guarantee a safe and healthy stay in Maputo and take full advantage of the city's exciting culture and attractions by being educated, adopting preventative measures, and being proactive about healthcare.

Maputo transportation systems

Using Maputo's transportation system is a must while visiting the city since it provides a variety of choices to suit different tastes and requirements. Regardless of your preference for the ease of taxi rides, the cultural diversity of public transit, or the freedom of renting a car, here is a detailed guide to traveling in Maputo:

Transportation: In Maputo, taxis are a common form of transportation. Although some are metered, it's customary to haggle over rates in advance. To guarantee safety and reasonable prices, use trustworthy taxi services or ones that are suggested by your lodging. Taxis are an easy and reasonably priced way to get around the city, particularly when traveling short distances.

Tuk-tuks: Tuk-tuks, which are three-wheeled vehicles that weave through Maputo's busy streets, provide a taste of the local way of life to travelers. They provide a distinctive, outside view of the city and are often used for short trips. Affirm your ticket in advance and take in the vibrant ambiance as you go across several areas.

Bus Services: Maputo's public bus system links several areas of the city. Buses are reasonably priced; however, they may be packed and have erratic timetables. It's best to confirm times and routes ahead of time and be ready for a more genuine local commute.

Vehicle Rentals: Renting a vehicle is a practical choice for anyone looking for freedom and adaptability. In Maputo, there are several local and foreign automobile rental firms. But be aware of the driving conditions, traffic laws, and parking difficulties in your area. When seeing sights outside of the city center, a rental car might be quite convenient.

Cycling and strolling: You may stroll about Maputo's key districts since they are designed with pedestrians in mind. Strolling about the city offers the chance to take in its lively atmosphere and find hidden treasures. Bicycle rentals are also available in several locations, providing a green and healthy option to explore the region.

Uber: Uber is available in Maputo, as it is in many other cities, and offers a practical and often more transparent alternative to regular taxis. You can conveniently follow your journey, hail a car, and make electronic payments using the app, which enhances the ease and safety of your transportation experience.

Fisheries and Boats: Maputo features canals that are navigable by boats and ferries because of its coastal position. Although these choices aren't your main everyday transportation, they may nonetheless make your trip more enjoyable by providing you with different views of the city and the Indian Ocean.

Considerations for Safety: When using public transit, particularly late at night, be cautious. Select stations that are busy and well-lit, and pay attention to your surroundings. Prevent theft by keeping valuables safe, especially while using public transit and in busy locations.

Traffic Conditions: There is a lot of traffic in Maputo, particularly during rush hours. Be patient and carefully plan your travels, particularly if you're using the road. Using trustworthy navigation applications is advised if you want to get around the city's streets quickly.

Etiquette in Culture: Observe regional traditions while traveling by car. When catching a bus or cab, wait in a polite line and exercise patience when navigating the busy tuk-tuk lines. Accepting these little cultural differences improves your experience in general and encourages good relations with the locals.

By taking advantage of Maputo's many transit choices, you may not only get where you're going but also fully experience the beat of the city, turning your travels into an essential part of the experience.

Language and Communication

A fascinating part of the trip is navigating Maputo's language and communication barriers, which provides a window into the vibrant cultural fabric of Mozambique's city. This is a thorough guide to encouraging good communication and appreciating this dynamic city's language diversity:

Status Translation: Mozambique's official language is Portuguese, which is extensively spoken in Maputo. Even though many people in the region, particularly in cities and popular tourist destinations, know a few basic Portuguese words, it will help you communicate more effectively and build relationships with the locals.

Diverse Languages: Mozambique has a diverse linguistic environment, with many indigenous languages being spoken across the nation. You could hear people speaking Shangaan, Tsonga, Ronga, and other languages in Maputo. Accepting this variety shows respect for the region's rich cultural heritage and adds a genuine element to your relationships.

Translation applications: To overcome linguistic hurdles, think about using translation applications. These resources may be very helpful for expedient translations or for interacting with non-native English speakers. Having a translation tool on your smartphone might make it easier for you to get around in daily settings.

Sensitivity to Culture: It is crucial to comprehend the cultural context of communication. Mozambicans place a high priority on manners and subdued communication methods. Spend some time extending polite greetings to others, such as "Bom dia" (good morning) and "Boa tarde" (good afternoon), and be willing to strike up a discussion to establish rapport.

English in City Environments: English-speaking people are more prevalent in Maputo's metropolitan districts and popular tourist destinations. Employees at hotels, restaurants, and other tourism-related businesses often speak English well. Nonetheless, low English competence may exist in more traditional or isolated locations.

Regional Accents: Although Portuguese is the universal language, knowing regional dialects might improve your ability to communicate. Acquiring a few sentences in the prevailing dialects might be valued by the community and could lead to more genuine encounters.

Social Areas and Cafés: Maputo's lively café culture offers great chances for informal discussions. Locals congregate in these areas often to mingle, and having cordial conversations may result in deep friendships. Don't be afraid to say "Olá" (hello) and start a conversation.

Respectful Gestures: In Mozambican culture, nonverbal communication is very important. Observe gestures, facial expressions, and body language. Kind gestures, like a grin or a nod, may imply warmth and transparency and promote productive relationships.

Regional Marketplaces: You may hone your language abilities and take in the real hustle and bustle of the city by navigating Maputo's vibrant marketplaces. Having cordial interactions with vendors—even if they are just little gestures—can provide special experiences.

Patience and Flexibility: When conversing, adopt a patient and adaptable demeanor. Although there may be linguistic obstacles, having a cheerful disposition and being open to change can help to ensure productive exchanges. The locals appreciate your effort, even if it's limited to trying out a few Portuguese words.

Maputo's communication and language skills are essentially the doorway to cultural immersion. Seize the chance to interact with people, exchange tales, and enjoy the distinct linguistic characteristics that add to this fascinating city's colorful mosaic.

Chapter 12

Day Trips from Maputo

Inhaca Island

Off the coast of Mozambique, Inhaca Island is a captivating jewel that entices with its immaculate beaches and abundant aquatic life. Travelers from all over the world are drawn to the island as it comes to life with a vivid energy when the sun sets on the turquoise seas.

You'll find a paradise of biodiversity strolling along the sandy shoreline, with unusual fish dancing under the surface and vibrant coral reefs. The marine reserve that envelops Inhaca is a monument to the marvels of nature, providing snorkelers and scuba divers with an up-close look at an underwater show.

As one travels further, the island's verdant surroundings become more apparent. Here, tropical flora flourishes due to the warm, humid air. The fragrant blend of spices and sea wind creates a sensory symphony that amplifies the pleasure of discovering the island's lesser-known areas.

The quaint communities of Inhaca Island, where the native way of life blends with the waves' rhythms, are the island's beating heart. Handcrafted goods and the day's fresh fish are on display at traditional marketplaces, giving visitors an insight into the islanders' way of life.

When day gives way to night, Inhaca becomes a haven for stargazers. When light pollution is at its lowest, the sky is transformed into a blank canvas covered with many constellations that inspire wonder and reflection.

Inhaca Island provides a diverse range of activities that capture the essence of this captivating region of the globe, whether you're looking for adventure under the waters, leisure on the beaches, or cultural immersion in the towns.

Island of Xefina

Tucked away in the blue embrace of an unidentified ocean, Xefina Island is a secret gem just waiting to be found. This remote oasis provides a haven far from the rush of the contemporary world, covered in a tapestry of emerald-green vegetation.

As you meander about the island, the sound of nature's symphony envelops you. A beautiful image is created by the vivid colors of tropical flowers and the towering palms that move softly in the air. Every step you take is met with an entrancing atmosphere infused with the pleasant scent of exotic blooms.

The shoreline of Xefina reveals an unspoiled beauty show. As far as the eye can see, ivory-white beaches are accompanied by the soft lap of glistening waves. Adventurers are drawn to quiet coves that promise quiet periods when the only noises are the murmurs of the sea and the occasional cry of a far-off bird.

There is an undersea realm waiting underneath the surface of the ocean. Similar to elaborate sculptures, coral reefs are home to a wide variety of marine life. A world of technicolor fish darting amid the coral may be seen while snorkeling, and the sea anemones' rhythmic swaying adds a captivating ballet to the underwater scene.

As one travels north, charming towns where time seems to stand still show the heart of Xefina. Warm-hearted locals tell stories about their island lifestyle, and lively marketplaces feature artisan goods and regional specialties. Each interaction is like a brushstroke on the cultural exchange canvas.

The island becomes a dreamscape as the sun sets, transforming the sky into shades of pink and orange. Above, a cosmic dance is taking place, with the nightly canvas glowing softly from the stars. It serves as a reminder that the marvels of the cosmos are ever-present, even in this isolated sanctuary.

Xefina Island welcomes travelers looking for adventure and peace to go into the center of paradise with its unspoiled scenery and well-balanced mix of nature and culture.

Excursion to Swaziland (Eswatini)

Traveling through the enthralling scenery of Eswatini, previously known as Swaziland, reveals a tapestry woven with natural beauty and cultural diversity. Tucked away in the center of Southern Africa, this little but charming country welcomes visitors to discover its distinct charm with an amazing fusion of history and contemporary.

The breathtaking Ezulwini Valley, which cradles the soul of Swazi culture, beckons as you travel across the undulating landscape. The countryside is dotted with traditional homesteads that are brightly painted with murals telling tales of perseverance and legacy. The Swazi people, renowned for their gracious hospitality, extend a warm welcome to you in a world where traditional practices converge with modern life's rhythms.

Experiences with native plants and animals at Mlilwane Wildlife Sanctuary reveal Swaziland's rich biodiversity. It is a haven for nature lovers. You may stroll or ride a horse along the meandering pathways, which provide up-close views of antelope, zebras, and a wide variety of bird species. The undulating hills around the sanctuary turn it into a refuge for those looking for peace in the embrace of wildness.

The lively marketplaces of Manzini are where the kingdom's colorful arts and crafts are brought to life. Beaded jewelry, colorful linens, and intricately woven baskets all highlight the exquisite workmanship that has been inherited throughout the years. Talking with local artists helps you connect with the creative community while also revealing the creativity that is infused into each item.

Swazi rites, steeped in history, provide a glimpse into the essence of Eswatini culture. Every year, the Reed Dance transforms into a celebration of femininity and solidarity as young maidens dress in brightly colored garments. The pulse of a country proud of its history is embodied by the rhythmic rhythms of the marimba, which reverberate through the atmosphere beyond simple music.

The Mkhaya Game Reserve cordially welcomes you to a nocturnal symphony as the sun sets. A distinct aspect of the animal realm is shown during night drives through the reserve, when elusive species come out of the shadows. Under the wide African sky, owl hoots and far-off lion roars meld into a melody that serves as a constant reminder that Eswatini's marvels don't stop at daybreak.

The famous Mantenga Cultural Village in the Ezulwini Valley serves as a live example of Swazi customs. Dance performances tell tales of love, conflict, and community while using vibrant costumes and rhythmic movements. Through its elaborate weaving throughout these performances, the Swazi way of life serves as a link between the past and the present.

A trip across Eswatini is a cultural voyage as much as a physical one. It's a journey into the cozy embrace of a kingdom where the sounds of tradition blend with the beat of the modern world to create a tune that stays in the hearts of those who are lucky enough to enter its domains.

Printed in Great Britain
by Amazon

37699210R00069